Love is the energy of the soul.
Love is what heals the personality. There is nothing that cannot
be healed by love. There is nothing but love.

−Gary Zukav, Seat of the Soul

Sway

Poems and Art

by

APRIL SIMONE KNIGHT

Giving Tree
Press

WWW.GIVINGTREEPRESS.COM

FIRST PUBLISHED BY GIVING TREE PRESS, INC. (2016)

PMB 3127, WEST TISBURY, MASS. 02575 U.S.A

To order this title, please visit the website: www.aprilsimoneknight.com

Library of Congress Cataloging-in-Publication Data

Knight, April, 1977-

Sway / by April Simone Knight.

ISBN (paperback) 978-0-578-17950-6

Cover Art:
Original Painting by Michael David Rottman
www.artmdr.com

For
my mother Anita Knight
and
my aunt Simone Reagor.

Thank you to the

Martha's Vineyard Center for Visual Arts (MVCVA)

for their help in the first publication of this book

and

my editor

Lynn VanAuken.

Dear Reader,

Over the past five years daily meditation has help me gain perspective on various events in my life during which I needed guidance. As time progressed so did my connection to Creator. I began writing the imagery and words that came to me in the form of poetry.

I have titled the book <u>Sway</u> because in moments of pure joy my physical body begins to sway with the energy that created it. I feel myself sway when I hold my children, when I'm in deep meditation, when I sing, write, paint and or see something beautiful. The feeling begins as a warmth in my bones and radiates throughout my body in a circular motion.

I hope this book finds you and inspires feelings that bring you closer to your blissful place.

With love,

April Simone Knight

Contents

Author Illustration: "Self Portrait"......8
Await Your Prose.....9
Vessel of Perfection.....10
Meet Yourself.....11
Be Still.....12
Song Bird.....13
Author Illustration: "Birds".....14
My Cup.....15
Be Free.....16
Proof of Heaven.....17
Resting Place.....18
Lambert's Cove.....19
It Dwells.....20
Author Illustration: "Woman".....21
Old Friend.....22
Speak Less.....23
I'll Be Waiting.....24
Oneness.....25
Dear Child.....26
Author Illustration: "Mother and Child".....27
Less.....28
Rope of Fear.....29
The Knot.....30
Healing.....31
Fulling Mill Brook.....32
Emotional Freedom.....33
Courage.....34
The Stream.....35
Helpers.....36
Author Illustration: "Holding Hands".....37
One Purpose.....38
Walls of the Spirit.....39
I See You.....40
In Love.....41
Creature of Earth.....42
Vast Exchange.....43
You Called?.....44
Light of Mercy.....45

Young One.....46
Good Morning Earth.....47
Author Illustration: "Lady Slipper".....48
To William.....49
Divine Form.....50
Toxic Spring.....51
Peak of Forever.....52
Broken.....53
Creation.....54
My Son.....55
Author Illustration: "Woman".....56
Heaven's Gate.....57
Author Illustration: "Prayer Hands".....58
Greetings Messenger.....59
Perfect Love.....60
Blessing.....61
Silence.....62
The Orchestra.....63
Angel.....64
Blessed Be the One.....65
True Self.....66
Maker of Justice.....67
Translucent Love.....68
It Is Enough.....69
True Love.....70
Author Illustration: "Flower".....71
Lakes Breath.....72
Scribe of Creator.....73

Await Your Prose

Broad strokes of eagerness bless my ready hand with warmth as I await your prose.

Words summoned by a certain true faith.

As your child I wait, still in the current of life.

Still in the moment of the motion of time.

Whisper your truth in images,

cast your seeds of knowing deep within my soul.

I will tend to them, sprouting the prose you wish.

With faithful water and courageous soil,

your bounty will bare fruit through me.

Words of the sweetest sort, scattered in the wind,

across the fertile hearts of those searching for the gift of your grace.

Vessel of Perfection

Sit, listen to the trickling of feelings,
Through your mind, down your core, dripping so sacred from
your ribs into your soul.

A mountain stream of sensation purred by nature's ground,
your own vessel of perfection.

Then feel God's love meet its final reservoir
only after it's filtered
through your earthly experience.

Be nourished by discomfort as if it is joy
for out of it
your strongest wishes are born.

Meet Yourself

You can meet yourself at any time of your choosing.
Just be sure it is someone you want to spend time with.
If you seek other company
know other seekers are as well.

Be Still

Just for this moment,
I will be still.

I will hear the music in your voice
Playing just for me,
Resonating joy of the deepest sort.

I'll roll in the essence of your divine attention,

I'll let go, be free in your vast space,
playful and yearning.

Releasing the physical words from their meaning,
I see you, not for what is next but for what is now.

Just for this moment,
I am more than still, I am yours.

Song Bird

I asked the song bird why she stopped singing
She said it wasn't the howling wind
Nor was it the broken nest

It wasn't the cold nights
or at someone's request

She had loved many masters
nibbled at their nose

Fluffed her feathers for beauty
as the story goes

She had babies of her own
raising one or two

Until it dawned on her
what was she to do?

She grew tired of the chorus
The song she always sang
The one that pleased no longer pleased

So she flew.

My Cup

I cannot save you,
My weary spirit has no
breath to call you back.

Your pain seeped in with fierce splinters, piercing the sensitive
landscape that once invited you.

My lungs, weak now, can't filter your toxin.

I beckoned you back, my throat ached,
calling your attention to truth, to love.

I call now only for peace.

You sipped from my joyful cup
as it drained, absorbed by your visceral emptiness.

But joy was a foreign pleasure, an unseeable cure.
Rage brought comfort, it wrapped your fears in a tomb of
perceived strength.
Dear one, the only true strength is love.

Light dimmed until dark silhouettes remained,
an apparition of affection, untouchable.

I fled, drifting away on gusts of hope infused with the scent of
happiness.

I took my cup with me.

Now, sustained by your own cup,
choose carefully what is in it.

Be Free

In this space floats creative life force,
from its high spring board it swirls playfully with grace
dives into the space of other kindred hearts.

Like wind across a path it gathers willing joiners
carrying them above the solid surface.

Dancing, floating, fulfilled at last not with the presence of the
wind, but with the joined lightness of the moment.

Be free with me for this experience.

Proof of Heaven

There is proof of heaven in your eyes.
A space between the past and future lit by desire.
Have we met before?

Perhaps on an autumn night at a Parisian building or at the base
of an ancient oak tree as children.

The bliss of you drenches my senses,
Capsizing in my internal landscape,
Giving way to a pulsing,
The heart beat of the universe now resides in me because of you.

Why do we linger in the shadows of discomfort?
Refusing the divine offering of our future.

Moments missed by the barreling momentum of fear
Only to be caught by the porous skin of another lover's touch
reminding us only of what was missed.

If time could retract I'd haul in my earthly hesitation and place
your soft form against mine.

Wrapping myself around you like a fertile vine.
Growing with you in this life as nature intended.

Resting Place

When I found you, my once loose intentions
attached to the delight of our union
like a seed which finally found its resting place.

It was the soil I craved, rich with intelligence I'd never known.

Gently pushed by the cosmic wind I rested on you,
in you,

as if angels whispered through the sparkle in your eyes

You are loved sweet one.

For the first time I believed it.

Lambert's Cove

I see you in the distance out of reach,
Decorated by the pink of God's light,
You call me to your angel arms.

 At first sight we begin our energetic merging.

An apparition of desire,
The taste of you, the smell.
Like the anticipation of a lover's kiss.
The hunger to be free in your vastness, to be one.

Your touch,
Altering the fabric of my skin to a deep blue silk,
Flowing endlessly.

Tides, spells cast by the moon, release the unease of the
past and future.

There is no time in your body, and now in mine.
Only the bliss of existence.

I go deeper, eyes closed,
an unrelenting faith fetches my thoughts.

Lapping my tender wounds with divine minerals
Cleansing the parts of me I cannot reach.

I am Grateful.

It Dwells

There is a place without a setting.

An area of knowing absent of thought.

It is silently vibrant and active,

Creation without form.

Aligning our process with each breath,

Beyond the blur of consciousness,

It dwells in all.

Old Friend

Old friend,

In your smile I see the radiance of
a thousand joyous hearts
Dancing by a cool night's fire.

Your gaze reaches deep into my caverns,
Bringing the ancient warmth that only our meeting ignites.

This isn't our first time soaked in the cosmic clarity of us,
Our past, our future.

In time, we'll no longer seek the exhilaration of contrast.

Our path to each other will be known.
Merged as the divine light intended.

As I have said for many lifetimes,

"I will see you again,

Until then, old friend."

Speak Less

Speak less my darling, think only about love.
How when we met my scent fertilized your soul's desire.

Touch more my love, like a drip of divine juice,
the salts of you on the tip of your most gifted instrument.

Do you see that less matters
when our hearts beat separate but as one?

I do.

Fear nothing but the bold abandonment of truth, of love,

its gift of living,

the cordial way it focuses our attention on God.

Our one truth, blissful purpose.

I'll Be Waiting

How did I lose you beneath the mask
or deep in the crevice of your pain?

Have I not loved you with all my being?

When you return,
I'll be waiting by the divine edge of our journey.

You know the place between the flicker of God's light and the
tree that birthed us.

Yes, I'll be there waiting,
experiencing again with crisp attention you tilting my face
up to your warmth
and kissing me with a thousand years of your love.

When your pain eases I'll be there.

Oneness

To understand is not to view from one's vantage point
but to feel the oneness of all
deep in your ribs.

Dear Child

Dear child,

Don't you know I molded you with a divine destiny.

Birthed with an emotional compass,

I gave you the freedom of joy,

the liberation of love,

and the courtship of desire.

Go now, remove all false pleasures
and seek the wealth of your birth.

Feel the light that reigns in your cells,

the ever lively spirit ignited by the

truth of my love.

Less

Nameless cast your widest net,
Gathering the bounty of all that nourishes.

Nameless become an essence,
A communicator through senses rather than words.

Nameless follow the craving of your desire
Amidst the distractions of circumstance.

Blameless cleanse the sour well that sustains you.

Drink again from the liquid sparkles of hope that once glistened
in your mother's eye upon first sight.

Nameless and Blameless walk free of spiritual injury.

Dissolve into being,
Bound by nothing,

Guided by the truth of love.

Rope of Fear

It is you who sees me clinging to my rope of fear,
Tightly suspended, a strong hold vantage point.

Admire my strength and look away.

Look away, Look away.

I cannot.

Admire my status and go away.

Go away, Go away.

I cannot.

Hold tightly here, you will see the strength it takes.

I will not.

Come observe my success.

**I see nothing but your aching hands,
my love.**

The Knot

Sweet one hold still while I loosen the knot of your suffering.

I see it buried deep within, twisted and tight
from the tugging of your pain.

Be still love, I'll soften the hardened mass with my kindness.

My strong good will inching into the center
massaging the string of loss.

It turns to silk,
smooth and shimmering it begins to slide,
releasing,
transforming.

Healing

Healing rests in the moments between thinking,
you just have to wake it up.

Fulling Mill Brook

Forget not the way in which the river flowed to this destination,
Revel in your journey winding,
Turbulent like the white water
rushing past jagged rocks
Undefeated.

You too are fluid, in motion,
gathering the landscape of your experience,
shifting with the forces of an angel's nudge.

Feel the river bed of the past and the constant seeking,
rushing of what is to come.

Flow and sparkle with gratitude for all gifts that are presented to
you in this abundant existence.

For when you meet your final reservoir
it will embrace you as it has the souls of all God's creations.

Emotional Freedom

Suffering seeks not to punish but to inform the spirit of its
deviation from the intended path.

It is of no use to ignore it, numb it, or resist it
for it will return until the course of emotional freedom is traveled.

Courage

I hang here on the one true branch of my courage.
Suspended and still I await your warmth to make me fluid.

For now I observe me, a constellation of a self
with bubbling desires and currents of imperfection

only visible by your light
and transformed by your grace.

The Stream

The stream of consciousness,

See not the force that sways the construct of this body.
Note the ever changing compositions on the bedrock of the soul,

The way the patterns of darkness infused with sparkles swirl,
Buoyant and flowing
with the energetic motion of the universal tide.

Calling to let go of all that blocks the freedom of such beauty.

To drift or row?

To plant or sow?

It is more simple.

For there is no question of action inspired by the stream.

There is only the admiration of its beauty,
The bliss of surrender to its organic divinity,

Transparent, yet visible,
Fixed, yet ever changing.

Teaching us of true impermanence.

Helpers

To You, loving kind soul who gives humans hope and plants seeds of courage with your bravery.

To You, who embodies how we all should see the world in its opportunities and glory rather than in its weakness and malice.

To You, messenger of spiritual strength and love.

To You, who sees a purpose beyond oneself, and taps into the integrity of the human spirit in all its splendor.

You fill the darkest days with light and gratitude. You are a spiritual conductor, who breathes life back into the hearts of those who have lost their way.

You are the potential of the human spirit at its best, for that you should walk with grace and love yourself.

One Purpose

Grace cast a golden net the day you were born,

Securing all that was now to be essential into one purpose.

Each soft fold of my skin is now a nest for your tiny glory,

A tender cavern to hold the moist droplets of your breath.

New one, how I relish your scent, the fragrance of tart milk
Wisps of your hair like the finest angels' down.

Sleep now as your journey will start
with my worship, my abundant care for your needs.

I promise to sow your seedling heart with all that is loving.

I promise to teach you hope with my smile,
selfless with my gaze.

Through you I see a mirror to heaven,

The Creator planted his gift within the walls of my womb.

I am now a holy vessel.

Walls of the Spirit

Fall away hard rock,
flake by flake from the walls of this spirit.

With every love, every act of kindness, your purpose is null.

When the softness of freedom is restored this story will
deafen fear and spark joy of the deepest sort.

Floating in a realm of self, above the constructed
to heavenly chaotic order.

Discovering at last that formality is an illusion of the unfaithful
spirit.

So it is with faith that I listen to the silent intelligence of this
moment, the wholeness of its offering.

I See You

I see you child, here before me
Yearning for a distraction from your suffering.

Scarring your most sacred landscape to exhibit your vulnerability.
It is only a shell.

An exterior surface to a cosmos of divine organization.
Which is you.

You are here before me, as a child of God.

My daughter,

My sister,

My kin.

Indeed there is love for you here,

Love that acts as a witness to your pain,

A compassion that props the burden off your heart.

Holding it above the lungs of the soul so it may gain its breath.

I see you child, here before me.
Can you feel me with you?

In Love

The dusk summons the last golden hues from the sky,
beneath the horizon.

You are with me watching the swallows dart atop the grass to
dine on the last mobile feast

You are with me.
It was here we fell in love.

Our toes stroked by the grass as we walked,
our skin aglow with the last of God's radiance.

Creature of Earth

Creature of earth summon to you peace just as the trees sway to divine music of angel's harps.

Creature of earth observe the vastness of your inner space gliding into depths of your eternal sea, weightless and carried by energetic tide.

Creature of earth withstand the friction of love for it offers with it the pulse of life.

Creature of earth see the grandiosity of miracles in each moment, the genetic history, the divine timing and revel in the inexplicable.

Creature of time offer thoughts and dreams that will transform and inspire.

Creature of time attach with deepest empathy to the scope of your life, offer not only your service but the imprint of your legacy on the fabric of cosmic evolution.

Creature of time realize the cosmic recruitment of you for the purpose of creation.

Creature of Creator be love in the wake of suffering and hold the truth of love's power at the root of all your actions.

Vast Exchange

Embark on the journey of breath,
a vast exchange of knowing.

For in this moment, all we are and were is stored in breath.

To breathe with devotion in our lungs
consciously adoring the air exhaled
we are giving all breathing creatures this capsule of affirmation.

You Called?

You called upon me
have you not?

Amidst your pain you question "Why."
Amidst your weeping you ask "Is it just?"

I can only say that my love for you follows no script.
No deliberate action of presentation to the trials before you.

There is no destination, there are only the trials of the soul,
determined by your ever evolving spirit.

Yes you, the one who beckons expansion, determines these trials.
You summon them as the powerful creator of your experience.

In each moment you are seeking a higher level of the spiritual
truth, your journey is your own and unique.

When the grass is thirsty it grows longer roots,
When the tree lacks sunlight it finds a new position.

So go now child, examine your own question.

Ask not "Why?"
Ask, "What does this tell me about my spiritual journey?"

Ask not "It is just?"
Ask, "Does this trial justify a new path?".

You will reemerge as you always do,
forever an apprentice of Holy Grace.

Light of Mercy

There is peace in this room,
between the man that sleeps and he who is awake.

The life that is with us, may motion to be forgiven one last time,
in one last breath.

He who tended with honest hopes of healing will be praised.

It may not be when the kindness is in action,
but when the wounded heart finds the tender light of mercy

in surrender,
one knows that God has blessed the healer and healed with the
gift of compassion.

A glimpse of oneness bound in time,
the fusion of two uniting through the virtue of humanity.

Young One

While you sleep young one
cradled in the fabric of softness

What world are we creating?

While you rest with light lids to cover your innocent eyes

What world are we creating?

As your skin catches the first warmth of sun

What world are we creating?

As you dream of the tenderness of your mother's breast

What world are we creating?

Good Morning Earth

Good morning earth
dew against your skin
dampening with the nurturance of angels sweat.

In these early rays the sun carries with it the cosmos,
dense warmth infused with timeless life.

Each beam stretching and gathering intentions of the day from
each divine waking soul.

The sleepy stirring of life, returning once again to their
instruments of action.

The coolness of temperature with the warmth of promise.

Early moments nourished by the state of wakening,
a state that until dissolved gives access to the infinite.

To William

You have departed dear friend,
at last free from the bounds of your physical nature.

I ask not that you delay your plans for eternity.
I ask that you place a wish in the hands of God on my behalf.

In your absence I will seek the compassion of your glance,
the hum of life in my bones as we spoke.

In your absence I will crave to be your reader, your audience and
your listener as I once was.

You see, while you were here the angels put their greatest gifts in
your pocket.

I ask that you place a wish in the hands of God on my behalf.

That is, the wisdom to feel these gifts in the elements of this earth,

the grace of your love in the clouds,
the sound of your presence in the wind,
and the warmth of your eternal spirit in my chest.

With this wisdom I may breathe without the shallowness of loss.

Divine Form

Speak with the compassion of an infant's touch,
before you stands the strands of divine form assembled into life.

Attend like a beam found amidst the clouds after a storm
before you stands the seeker of connection

Act with the grace of an angel's intention,
before you stands a creation of God.

An infinite being set forth to create with you and for you,
adoringly under the grace of all that was before and and all that
will be.

Toxic Spring

Oh toxic spring of thoughts,
I wish your well would dry up.

Self love will stop your flow,
here I have found it.

Floating atop the current of appreciation.

Peak of Forever

I meet you there at the peak of forever,
in the abundant golden glow of promise,

Follow me, you whisper.

Resistant, I'm guided by your love's depth.
In this warmth I surrender not only my fears but deny the gentle
tugging of doubt.

For in you I see curiosity of innocence,
the glory and power of evolutions finest work.

Your gaze across the distant view, I watch.
I see you breathless, dazed by the mystic powers of reverence.

Observing you whole, I'm complete.

Broken

Broken, before you I stand
beyond the grace of compassion's mending.

I dread now not the basic fear of loneliness
but the primal rejection of self–love.

I've known the darkness of a wounded soul better than most.
It is not death I fear now.

It is the absence of this love, pure and transformative.

Reject me not, I pray.

Against the currents of thought, see me beyond this moment.

The gift of tenderness that lay at your feet,
summoning mercy of the greatest form,

Cradle me, you are my wish.
See good through pain, you are my salvation.

A glimpse of heaven's healing on earth.

Creation

The marvelous creation of mass,

ounce per ounce flooding, building on the synergy of thought.

To be nothing and then something.

To be absent then present.

A magic merging of chemistry, the glue of cosmic past and
intentional future.

How can one deny the magic?

My Son

The light flickers on your new skin,
playing in the warm sun
I realize I've never know such surrender.

It is now that I meet God,
in the company of tiny you.

The spaciousness of my chest now encompasses
all that you will touch, the trials and joys of your life will be
bound to my heart like the seal of an ancient king.

I pledge my eternal love,

beyond the limit of possibilities,

at the feet of the creator.

I surrender to this certain mercy that when life beckons me to act
on my behalf solely I will remember this pledge.

The eternal gift bestowed on me this day,
you my son.

Of my flesh,

Of my womb,

Of my heart.

Heaven's Gate

In the moments of waking I stretch my
Spirit beyond heaven's gate

Ascending through the layers of light and darkness into
the pearl ethos.

The brightness of your grace cast a cloak of resolve around the
being called self.

Free, no longer me.

Now I'm the harmony of an Angel's harp,
activated by a current of divinity.

Submerged in a pool of surrender, floating, carried above the
bedrock of feelings toward bliss.

I am one but many,

Full but unoccupied.

With gratitude
I'm swaddled in joy,
returning with a piece of heaven residing still inside of me.

I offer this to you.

Greetings Messenger

Greetings messenger,
before me again, amber red feathers, exquisitely perfect in design.
My soul takes flight with you, across the green field.

Greetings messenger,
Your delicate curves, rich colors,
I loose my rigid expectations in my study of your flawless form,
your scent, your display of beauty for my internal delight.

Greetings messenger,
massive living wood transcends the boundary of earth and sky,
the scent of life in your bark, encased by the texture of living
armor.

Living warrior teach me strength,
Passive witness teach me patience,
Old soul pull me in to feel the rings of time within your belly.

Share with me your message,

I will listen.

Perfect Love

Perfect Love find me,

Beyond the past of dissolved hopes,

Across the dry planes of forgiveness.

Perfect love find me,

Ready to release the grip of thoughts that no longer serve me,

preparing for the journey to one light,

one expansion,
for you are the catalyst,

the chemical counterpart that will ignite
the divine fire within my soul.

A boundless,

raw,

unrelenting

Love.

Perfect.

Blessing

In this circle of eternal faith we are witness to
an untouchable but brilliantly present bond.

With a silent hold,
Together we cast our wish,
Our gratitude,
To all that was and all that is before us.

Beyond the table that hosts us and
the offering that is before us we acknowledge that it is only by
divine grace that we are nourished.

As we feast on the bounty of this moment we are touched by
peace through the worship of our life family and our holy family.

Silence

On the edge of thoughts, words, and prediction is a reservoir.

It lies still with peace, glassy calmness acting as a mirror to the heavens.

The depth unknown, the internal landscape only accessible by silence.

The Orchestra

Be light with deep breath
for all that is yet to come is awaiting your cue.

Behind the heavy curtain of impatience is an
orchestra of extraordinary measure,

in tune for your deepest pleasure,
a flawless harmony, your soul's pitch.

Instruments of pure elements, played by angel's breath.

Be light,
for all that is yet to come is awaiting your cue,

Not a cue of gesture, a cue of faith.

Angel

You are here,

Indeed you are.

It is not the scent of you,
your form or voice.

It is the beam of your soul's glow in my chest,

warming the absent place since you left.

You are here,

Indeed you are,

unbound,

guided by strands of golden light
jetting with lively purpose
to my awareness.

Blessed Be the One

Blessed be the one with no ideas of absolute,

Bound by threads of surrender to Creator's truth.

Blessed be the one who has carefully crafted intentions of loving
without expectations.

Acting to serve others, absent of personal gain other than the joy
of loving oneself.

Blessed be the one that can decipher the true purpose of a present
moment.

Offering access to the magic of experience,
living as one,
breathing as one

and feeling the pulse of all that lives
within the walls of the ribs.

True Self

Call on your true self,
the one that sees past desires of physical manifestation
the one that calls on the wisdom of the spectacular
the one that knows the journey beyond words
and calls the stepping stones of evolution to your feet.

Call on your true self.

Maker of Justice

Maker of justice
who do you serve?

Weaving your cloaks of truths so tight that you can't feel the rain.

For in the moments of true dishonor,
truth becomes just a construct of personality,

the judgement of one with no true authority.

It is not restriction of freedom that acts as salvation,
it is discovery of the spaciousness within self that acknowledges
our connection and the action that harmed.

Translucent Love

Speak through the silence of eternity,

mend this human heart with the threads of compassion and understanding.

Show the broken the path to resemblance,

Energize the weak with the effervescent delight of health.

Cleanse the palate of those who crave contempt.

Before this time expires,

the actions during the trials of this great journey

will either push you closer to the translucent love of Creator's

womb or draw you away to a new journey whose trials will bend

you with greater force.

It is Enough

It is enough to know the glory of purpose,

for it is infused in the clarity of a desirable scent,

the warmth in the chest at the thought of love.

It is enough to see beyond the current day,

and dissolve self into the timeless,

the connected and prosperous field of eternity.

True Love

True love brings you to the altar of your soul,

bowed in deep surrender, the self dissolves.

Lake's Breath

Under this tree, greeted by the lake's breath, I am,
Noticing only the stillness of this moment, I am.
Free of the beckoning of life, I am.

Drawn to this earth with the same magnetic ease of all God's
creation, I am.

Part of this, I am.
Practicing gratitude of connection to all this, I live.

Scribe of Creator

A soul's purpose can't be edited by the doctrines of a culture or
the wishes of others,

The revisions of one's mission take shape only at the hands of the
scribe of Creator, you.

The story forms around the truth discovered in each moment
that passes,

In each human life lies the key to the soul's truth.

In the active practice of deep witness, one blossoms and the
beauty of the spirit is revealed.

This is undeniably the magic of life.

In turn,
the scribe's contribution to the evolution of the collective soul,
the inexplicable vibrational record of humankind.

Author Biography

April Knight is a counselor, educator, consultant, writer, publisher, artist and singer.

April is a Kripalu trained Reiki practitioner, Theta Healing practitioner and has done extensive studies in contemporary spiritual thinking and healing arts. She is a regular participant in yoga, meditation, guided imagery and community blessings.

She enjoys being part of her church community, being a mom, cooking for others and activities near the ocean. She lives on Martha's Vineyard in Massachusetts.

www.aprilsimoneknight.com